Creative Confidence: Learn To Harness the Power of Creativity

The Complete Guide on How to Use Creative Confidence in Your Everyday Life

Alan Kensington

PUBLISHERS NOTES

This publication is intended to provide helpful and informative material. It is not intended to diagnose, treat, cure, or prevent any health problem or condition, nor is intended to replace the advice of a physician. No action should be taken solely on the contents of this book. Always consult your physician or qualified health-care professional on any matters regarding your health and before adopting any suggestions in this book or drawing inferences from it.

The author and publisher specifically disclaim all responsibility for any liability, loss or risk, personal or otherwise, which is incurred as a consequence, directly or indirectly, from the use or application of any contents of this book.

Any and all product names referenced within this book are the trademark of their respective owners. None of these owners have sponsored, authorized, endorsed, or approved this book.

Always read all information provided by the manufacturers' product labels before using their products. The author and publisher are not responsible for claims made by manufacturers.

Published by:
SPEEDY PUBLISHING LLC
40 E MAIN ST, #1156
NEWARK, DELAWARE 19711

Paperback Edition

Manufactured in the United States of America

WHAT YOU WILL LEARN IN THIS BOOK
How This Book Will Help You and Why

Being insecure about your appearance is no joke; it can greatly influence your self-esteem in a negative fashion. If you are unhappy with the skin you are in, you live under a cloud of self-doubt. This book will guide you on the right path to success on how to boost your confidence and raise your self-esteem.

TABLE OF CONTENTS

Publishers Notes		**2**
What You Will Learn In This Book		**3**
Table of Contents		**4**
Dedication		**5**
1	First Step Is To Learn To Be Happy With Who You Are	**7**
2	Know Thyself : The Critical Factor	**13**
3	Talk, Talk & More Talk Make You Confident & Then Some	**20**
4	Become A People Magnet	**26**
5	Social Anxiety : How To Rise Above It	**30**
6	Just For The Guys : Why That Is So Important	**38**
The Most Important Thing You Can Do To Spread The Word		**44**
About The Author		**46**

Dedication

Be yourself and be confident! I dedicate this book to everyone that's struggling to make themselves a better person!

> *"Calm mind brings inner strength and self-confidence, so that's very important for good health."*

Dalai Lama

1   First Step Is To Learn To Be Happy With Who You Are

...

Being insecure about your appearance is no joke; it can greatly influence your self-esteem in a negative fashion. If you are unhappy with the skin you are in, you live under a cloud of self-doubt. Furthermore, you compare your features unfavorably to other people and do not feel that you are acceptable. Learning how to gain body confidence can increase your sense of self-worth.

At times, the fact that the perfect, airbrushed image of people that the media provides is virtually impossible to replicate in the form of a human probably escapes you. In the back of your mind, you half understand that you have been measuring yourself up against extreme ideals.

Nonetheless, you have succumbed to the pressure shoved in your direction by society to believe that you are faulty.

Do not feel bad about being taken in by the false concept of beauty that is presented via the television, magazines and beauty industry. You are certainly not alone in having fallen foul of Mother Nature's quest to send you forth into the world with a total acceptance of yourself as a whole.

Like countless other people, you almost certainly find it hard to fight against the tide of information offered regarding how, apparently, you are supposed to look.

In order to be happy being you, it will help if you start looking at the reality of the beauty business. Companies selling cosmetics, clothing, and plastic surgery procedures and so on want to generate money. The only way they can do so is to convince the public that their services are required.

Telling you that you are already beautiful would make them redundant. However, if they inform you that you need corrective surgery, makeup to cover your faults and clothing that makes you look acceptable they are likely to obtain your attention.

Furthermore, the media supports the beauty industry. Advertisements on the television telling you to buy exercise equipment, cosmetics, and other paraphernalia designed to help you primp and preen, provide funding. At the same time, magazines rely on a similar method of making money to help keep them afloat. You see, it is in the media's best interests to push the beauty industry down your throat.

There is nothing wrong with you

Numerous magazines produce articles that are supposed to help you feel confident about your appearance. However, they tell you that to increase self-esteem, you must go on a diet, fix your face, and transform your hair. Unfortunately, the only message that your brain receives after reading such content is that you are faulty. You can be forgiven for thinking that you are substandard and should attempt to sculpt yourself into the image you are instructed to adopt.

People fall for the absurd message that they are defective since they want to be accepted by others. Humans have an innate need to belong, which is why they go to great lengths to fit in with their peers and do what they imagine is expected of them. No one wants to be ostracized or embarrassed because he or she does not adopt a fashionable appearance.

However, it is improbable that you will be rejected by anyone that matters to you if your eyes are spaced further apart than is fashionable and you have wrinkles on your forehead. In other words, the idea that there is a need to look a certain way is a farce. You can exist perfectly well as the unique individual that you are, without anything dreadful happening to you, despite not having liposuction or wearing supersonic mascara.

Nevertheless, absorbing such a message is tough when you have spent years listening to the advice of the beauty industry and media. Letting go of old ideas that have thwarted your attempts to thrive might take time.

Having taken the first step toward self-acceptance by recognizing how you are bombarded with unrealistic images, you can move on to the next stage of your quest, which is discovering genuine beauty.

What is genuine beauty?

Beauty cannot be defined by current trends since they are ever changing ideals. What was fashionable a hundred years ago was different from what society considers attractive now. Furthermore, people whose appearance fit the existing concept of beauty might easily be deemed unattractive by such standards in a few years' time. Therefore, genuine beauty, which is not guided by trends, is enduring.

True beauty has little to do with size, weight, how long someone's legs are, or any other elements used as measuring sticks to define attractiveness according to contemporary ideals.

The Venus De Milo and the Mona Lisa have always been considered beautiful; yet, their features certainly do not look fashionable. You do not have to alter yourself; just as such enduring icons of beauty need not be changed.

Let go of the concept that you need to modify yourself in order to be considered attractive and you are half way to self-acceptance.

Accepting the whole of yourself

Occasionally, forward thinking beauticians and fashion advisers tell people that instead of attempting to conceal unfashionable features, they should emphasize physical aspects that are trendy.

While such a concept is far more empowering than being told that you should focus on negativity, the unspoken message is still that parts of you are not up to scratch. The idea is that if you heighten features thought of as positive, your, so called negative features will not stand out.

In order to increase your self-esteem, you can use cosmetics, clothing, or whatever you like to help you. However, do not utilize such materials if you do so as an attempt to diminish yourself in any way. By all means, celebrate the joy of color, creative design, and the individuality that fashion can provide, but think of it in terms of a complementary, playful addition to your style.

Likewise, if you want to eat healthy foods, do so because you want to be physically strong and feel great. Do not go on a diet in order to emulate skinny models. Part of the reason that most diets do not work long term is that losing weight for the wrong reason engenders a feeling of misery. It is painful to feel as though you are unacceptable and must make attempts to be considered satisfactory.

Change the way you think

You can only become happy with your features if you stop thinking about yourself negatively. The more you become aware about how you have been thinking in a less than constructive manner regarding your appearance, the easier it will be to catch such thoughts in motion and set them straight.

When negative thoughts occur, remember what you have learned about the beauty industry, and about how genuine beauty is not always fashionable. Furthermore, base decisions to alter any part of your life on the desire to be joyful since joy is the ultimate low self-esteem buster.

2   KNOW THYSELF : THE CRITICAL FACTOR

. . .

While on the outside you might portray yourself to others one way, which you are deep inside, might be someone altogether different. As you journey through life, the real you will rise to the surface, now and then, jostling for position with the you that is needed for mere survival.

Who you are at birth is either both nurtured and allowed to bloom, or it is at risk of being stifled. Out of necessity, individuals follow the systems of the world. There are certain rules of conformity to be followed, some by law. How a person performs is based on criteria set out by caregivers and educational institutions. Focus is put on that which demands the most attention at the time. The world's commodity, for the most part, is money and achievement and all individuals fall prey to its grasp, sometimes at the cost of losing themselves.

Who are you deep inside? Have you thought that question through? Do you know the answer? Do you feel as though the you deep within the surface is calling out to be released? If you have been functioning for the most part in your true self, are you thriving? Is life working for you, or could you use some guidance?

Who Are You?

Deep inside you, beyond the practical self, is your spiritual self. From it stems a set of beliefs, motivations, values and core skills. These come with your DNA. They provide the foundation for your drive, feelings, and personal motivation. They all serve to form your personality.

When these core traits are in alignment with how you live your life, you blossom. When you are not using the gifts and talents you were born with, you are prone to frustration. When you are called to act or participate in something that doesn't align with the deeper you, you may feel deeply troubled or dissatisfied, even when feeling troubled makes little sense to the situation at hand.

Who you really are inside strives to emerge. It longs for expression and acceptance or even applause. The way you act, the books you like to read, your hobbies and your sense of style are all a reflection of the true you, when expressed in honesty. This true you might be referred to as your archetype.

You may strongly veer in the direction of a predominant archetype or you may be a blend of many. Each archetype has its strengths and weaknesses. Each has a dark side and a light side. The dark side is that which is filled with doubt, frustration and disillusionment. The light side is where your gifts are engaged and there is flow. When you are thriving you will feel satisfied, fulfilled and will be productive.

The Artist Archetype

One archetype is that of the artist. Inside every soul is an apportioned ability to create. There are those who can paint anything they visualize. There are those who can build a sculpture that is undeniably lifelike.

There are those who enjoy the process of cake decorating, but for whom the finished product will barely stand up against the decorated cakes of a local grocery store. Then there is the person with very little artistic skill, but who appreciates viewing fine art, attending magnificent plays and who has a well-developed ear for music.

The true artist archetype is creative. She longs to make what she sees in her mind come to life. She longs to twirl and dance with her whole body. She seeks solace in the smooth sounds of her guitar. Her artistic flair longs to break forth in new and unimagined ways, sometimes surprising even herself.

Are you an artist? Does creativity stir your soul?

While your artist archetype is inborn, it also becomes conditioned by your environment and experiences. Contextually, who you are at any given moment depends on how you choose to adapt to the situation at hand. You can either draw from your artist archetype or choose not to.

The contextual process of adaptation often becomes necessary in order to function in society, and some behaviour become habitual. Adaptation provides a means of protection, but conforming can suffocate the aspiring artist inside. Adaptation or suppression can dull a person over time.

The Artist Archetype and Life Existence

Though many people can create, only a portion will make a career out of their creativity. The practical needs of life get in the way. There are bills to pay and mouths to feed.

For that reason, many individuals will spend a large portion of their day in a career that is vastly removed from their artist side. We've all heard of the person who is a server by day and night club singer by night. That may work for some. They may even enjoy the dual role as one role feeds the other emotionally and socially.

For the artist archetype that seeks to make a living from her talents, the road can be tough. Some have been taught to believe that the hallmark of a true artist is her capacity to create in the face of poverty—to be a starving artist living under the mystic power of creativity while struggling to pay the week's bills.

This, however, is no way to live. The idea that ongoing suffering somehow engenders greater works of art is actually a myth. Suffering results in a depletion of energy. It starves the spirit and reduces creativity.

The Artist Archetype thrives when her intuitive intellect is engaged. The susceptibility to the shadow side requires the artist keep vigil to live outside it. When the shadow threatens to close in, it serves the artist to see it as a call for healing and support.

Living the Thriving Life

If you have felt the artist deep within you has been quiet for far too long, consider giving it attention. This can take form in several ways:

Dabble: You may be creative but can't pinpoint one specific art form you love more than another. You don't necessarily have to limit yourself. Try jewellery making, sketching, stained glass work or flower arranging. Offer to help a local theatre company make props. Expose yourself to different medium and discover what makes your heart beat.

Learn: Workshops abound to learn new skills or practice existing ones. You can keep your day job and take a workshop in your spare time.

Give: You've been given the artist archetype so that you can use it to bless the world. Create and give the world a taste of the creativity that springs forth. Present your works to the world.

If you are a fulltime artist, here's how to keep yourself in balance and thriving:

Own It: Own your archetype. Believe in yourself. Be convinced that you have artistic purposes to fulfil, and focus on releasing it daily.

Stay Vigil: Recognize your shadow side and equip yourself with tools to expel it. See its emergence as a call for healing and balance.

Network: Find a like-minded community to share with. Seek inspiration from other artists. Try using a coach or agent. Ask for help or advice when needed. Promote others and their work and ask them to do likewise.

If you have seen yourself in any of the above, ask yourself what you can do today to begin living more in your personal archetype. What must be left behind? What must change? Where must you spend more time in order to gain the momentum and balance your soul craves?

Choose to embrace, with unshakable certainty, which you are. Find where you fit. Don't live with frustration another day. Give your gift to the world and thrive.

3   Talk, Talk & More Talk Make You Confident & Then Some

. . .

Being a good conversationalist is a skill that is valuable in both business and personal settings. Knowing who you are, what you like, and what you excel at will help you to become a good conversationalist and will help you to paint the image that you want others to see. The other side of the coin in being a good conversationalist includes knowing the right questions to ask others in order to keep conversations going.

Your conversation and the image you portray may be communicated in-person, through print, or through the social media tools you use. A major form of conversation today takes place by texting, commenting on status updates, and email. People can "meet" through Facebook and feel as though they've had a face-to-face conversation. What you say and how you say it matters.

Conversation Creates Image

The subjects you choose to discuss and the words you use to discuss them communicate who you are. You can vary the picture you want portrayed to suit the circumstance, though. Knowing which "cards" to pull at the right time will make you a good communicator. One time you might pull your "parent" card, another, your "professional" card, and another time, your "hobby" card. Fit the subject to the circumstance. Alternatively, you may fluctuate between serious conversation for one group and jesting and humor for another.

If you are using conversation to "brand" yourself, you will want to choose the type of personality you want others to see. For instance, if you want to be seen as an optimist who is also very down-to-earth, your social media status updates should be uplifting and positive; while at the same time should show a few personal tidbits that show your human nature.

Importance of Questions

People generally love talking about themselves and key questions become good prompters for initiating good conversation. Key questions are also helpful for steering conversations in the direction you'd like—possibly toward an opportunity to highlight your own successes. Knowing the right questions to ask can also help you more quickly zero in on the type of information you want to gain from another person, without sounding intrusive.

You may be on the receiving end of keen conversationalists that is armed with his own set of questions. You won't be caught off guard if you've done your homework and prepared a few preferred answers. Choose answers that will give the listener the best picture of who you are, what you value, and how you approach life or work.

Good Key Questions

So what are good key questions to ask yourself or others?

Here are a few examples with explanations:

1. What are your favorite hobbies/activities/fun things to do?

Sharing about a few of your personal interests will help paint a picture of your personality in the minds of others. By giving the question forethought, you can make sure your answer paints the right kind of picture, preferably an exciting one.

If you love the outdoors, for instance, instead of sharing about your backyard bird watching hobby, you might want to talk about an interesting hiking trail you've spotted birds on, instead. Conversation that points to more general hobbies or tourist spots create good jumping off points for further dialogue.

2. What is your passion? What makes you feel fulfilled?

The answer to this question should be adapted to the situation at hand. If you are asked this question in a job interview, for instance, the best answer should be job related rather than about something you do for fun on the weekends. You might share that you love meeting new clients and closing deals, rather than sharing your love of winemaking. Of course, in a social setting, a variety of interests can be shared.

3. What motivates you or gives you energy?

The things that give you the most fun and energy might be quite uninteresting to others. If you're fortunate, others will share your excitement. If they do, you can have fun with the conversation. If, on the other hand, it seems others don't understand what you do or if they don't seem interested, don't be apologetic. Demonstrate your enthusiasm.

Do try to put an interesting spin on your story and keep it short in cases where others aren't following. Don't criticize others for not having an equivalent level of interest in what you find interesting. Find out what they do that is interesting to them and let them take over the conversation.

A few other questions might include the following points:

What in your personal or professional life are you are most proud of?

What is going well for you?

What are your personal or professional strengths?

What do you want others to know about you?

Editing your answers to suit the situation is useful. Before answering a question, ask yourself why the question is being asked in the first place. Ask clarifying questions if you'd like more specific guidance before giving your answer.

Doing so will help keep you from walking into a trap or saying something you might regret. Answer questions with the information you feel is important for others to know, and leave out unimportant or confusing information.

Be Interactive, Not Longwinded

There's a saying, "People don't care how much you know until they know how much you care." It is important to show the person you're speaking with that you understand what is being said, that you get the point, and that you care.

You will show you care if you keep the dialogue two-way. You might be an expert on a certain subject, but unless you're being asked to give a speech, resist the urge to be longwinded or to dominate the conversation. Being a good conversationalist means you are effective in creating interactive dialogue. That means taking as much interest in the viewpoints of others as in your own points.

Becoming a good conversationalist is important both socially and professionally. Put some thought into how you interact with people both in person and online. Prepare your personal brand by answering a few key questions such as those listed above. Show others you care by interacting, stay respectful, and you'll do a good job! The last thing you ever want to do is air your dirty laundry online. Remember, once it is out there it is always out there. You can't delete it, once it has hit cyber world there is not going back.

4   Become A People Magnet

. . .

Mother Teresa was admired for her selfless efforts to ease the pain and suffering of the poorest of the poor in the slums of Calcutta. Everyone can't help but feel awe at the millions of dollars Bill Gates has given away to charities. So many wish they could be as successful of neighbors that seem to attract wealth without doing much to acquire it.

But this power, this magnetism doesn't come from years of training or experience. No school ever teaches you how to develop grace or charm to woo the opposite sex or influence others to do what you want them to do. As a householder you've found it difficult to inspire your spouse and children to follow your example. Just because you don't want junk all over the kitchen counters does not mean you can persuade them to stop dropping it all there.

What you fail to realize is that the source of personal magnetism doesn't come from a large bank account, your status on the job or the position of power you hold in your community. That ability to influence others comes from within the heart and the mind. Personal magnetism comes from the development of a caring attitude that looks out to help others. Those who have it succeeded in subduing their selfish nature long before they became influential.

To develop personal magnetism, the ability to attract others and influence them starts with taking a few simple steps to control your inner tiger.

Take Possession of the Self

Your mind is a powerful tool. Unfortunately, few people learn to control the jumble of thoughts that cross their minds every second. They have no sense of direction. Their minds are unfocused, undisciplined. An undisciplined mind has no foundation on which life goals can be built. Influential people attract simply because they know what they want and know where they are headed. Before you can hope to influence anyone else, you need to have a vision of what you want from life. You need to take possession of that amazing computer in your head, instead of merely drift like the masses do.

Imagination Rules the World

The power of imagination is enhanced when there is a clearly defined goal to shoot for. People are naturally attracted to anyone who can solve problems effectively and efficiently through the power of imagination and creativity. Think of the words of the R. Kelly song, I Believe I Can Fly - If I can see it, then I can do it. If I just believe it, there's nothing to it... Just see it in your head and do it!

Power Personalities Attract

Successful leaders don't associate themselves with negative minded people. They don't allow themselves to get dragged down by the constant bad news the media broadcasts every day. Such news sells, but does not lift the human spirit or provide the incentive to make changes. So many have a negative opinion of themselves as they were programmed to think that way. If you seek to develop attractive qualities, you need to associate with successful people. Success comes from the development of a mastermind group working toward a single goal for the benefit of all.

An Appreciation for Life

Successful people live life to the fullest as they know that life is short. They smile more. They project warmth and concern to everyone they meet. It's this genuine warmth that attracts people. You like to associate with someone who keeps a positive attitude even in the face of trouble. If you're not laughing and finding joy in every moment of your existence, you're not really alive.

The source to developing personal magnetism starts with you. No outside methods can help you develop the character that attracts. No drug, no vaccine, no psychiatrist or psychologist will ever help you find your life's purpose and work towards it. Personal magnetism starts from within you. Once you improve that, you will naturally exude charm and grace.

5 Social Anxiety : How To Rise Above It

...

Are you living a life of constant fear? Are you living a life of constant fear of your fear? How many times have you wished for something only to be dismayed and held back by your social anxiety?

We all want to be successful in life but there are times when the outside world can be overwhelming for some people. This can be something they have dealt with constantly since they were young or it can be triggered by an event in their lives that just pushed them too much and all of a sudden it was just overwhelming, and suddenly they feel fear. In this chapter we will explore that feeling.

Your life can be changed and the help you need is going to come from the most unlikely person: yourself. All you need is a slight push out of the door.

This is not a magical pill that will give you seven unstoppable tactics to overcome social anxiety in a minute, but it is rather a framework for how you yourself can start and continue to change into the person that you have always wanted to be.

The change can be slow, the change can be hard, but if you stick to the basic principles conveyed in this chapter you will notice slight changes in your life that push and lead you on the right track forward towards the new story of your new life.

1. Set goals.

Setting goals is an obvious, yet very important first step that should not be overlooked. You have to set goals for yourself and for what you want to accomplish. This includes both major long term goals and minor short term goals.

A long term goal might be that you want to see yourself as a social, talkative and charming person; while a short term goal might be that you start off the whole process by simply learning how to say "Hi" to strangers in your local grocery shop.

You can apply this sort of goal setting wherever you are in your development, no matter how much your social anxiety has hampered you so far in your everyday life. Bring out pen and paper and put down your goals in writing right now.

2. Small chunk your way forth.

Small chunk your goals, and do not expect too much of yourself at once. This attitude will give you poise and confidence in your endeavor, and is actually an important step in any undertaking, be it in skill requirement (learning how to play an instrument for example) or in a business venture.

You did not become what you are today over a night, and you will not become what you truly are and can be over a night. Even Mozart had to learn how to play a scale before he could start composing concertos.

Small chunking your goals will give you a better perspective of what you have to do, and it will make sure that you do not get overwhelmed by all the major goals that you have set for yourself.

Have a plan for the way up to the mountain top, but stay focused on the next step right in front of you. As long as you have clearly defined and set your goals in Step 1, you do not have to worry about following the wrong paths.

3. Expand your comfort zone.

We all, as humans, have our comfort zones in life and they do have their purposes. Issues arise when we get too comfortable in a specific behavior and avoid taking any perceived risks at all. Without strive towards something more in life, there would be no development at all; human civilization itself would have been stuck in a constant stone age and nothing new would ever have been invented, learned or created.

Whatever your current comfort zone is, pushing out of it will be hard, but it most definitely will be good for you. If you push too far at once you will get overwhelmed, but if you stay close to the shore in the beginning and slowly expand what you are comfortable with you will notice that the things that were once hard for you have become an everyday habit.

In the beginning when you start off by saying "Hi" to the cashier in your local grocery store you may experience anxiety, and it might even be that you are unable to utter a single word. But when you return back home again, there will still be something good that you can take with you from the interaction. For example, the fact that you even stepped out from your home and went to a public place is an indication that you are moving ahead.

Your focus on your next goal lets you be free of other issues that you are not even considering at the moment. Going out to the grocery store the next time, you may notice that you are still unable to say *"Hi"* to anybody, but this time you might manage to keep eye contact, nod and smile at the cashier.

Whatever your goals are, you will notice small advancements in your development if you actually push yourself to do something that is slightly uncomfortable. The anxiety might still be around, but when you calm yourself down and analyze the steps that you have taken you will certainly find some small improvements that you can hold on to and affirm.

You will be amazed by how fast you can expand what you are comfortable with when you do it in a slow and steady way.

4. Stay process oriented, not result oriented.

This step is one of the most important ones, and also one of the hardest, not to understand, but rather to actually embody and live by. We are all taught from a young age that once we accomplish something we have a right to feel good.

Once we perform well on a test in school, or once we finish a project at work. This kind of result oriented worldview will be of little help for you in your development towards being a happier and mentally stronger person.

When an individual is process oriented his or her focus lies not on the results that certain action lead to, but rather on the actions themselves.

This is easier understood if you consider the example with setting up a goal of saying "Hi" to all the employees in a grocery shop. You might pump yourself up and actually manage to speak up and greet one of the workers, only to be met by silence and a frown. Holding on to a result oriented focus in this case will only set you up for defeat.

It is important to remember that you cannot control anybody else's reactions towards you. The positive side of this is that you yourself do not have to be controlled by anybody else's reactions either, and that nobody in the whole world has any right at all to your thoughts, feelings and actions.

In a process oriented view all you derive your validation from are your own thoughts and actions, that is: once you have actually managed to speak up and say "Hi" your goal is accomplished and you have all the right in the world to be happy about your progress. Reactions are irrelevant to your happiness and progress. Once you realize this, you will feel more joyful in your everyday life.

5. Get in touch with like-minded people.

Getting in touch with like-minded people does not mean that you will simply find people who have the same issues that you have and disregard their outlook on life. People who like to dwell upon their problems without ever trying to overcome them will have a negative effect on your development. It is very easy to fall into complacency when one is surrounded by people that are not interested in changing and growing as a person.

Be on a lookout after individuals that are on the same journey as you are, and that are constantly striving towards improving and developing. If you are unable to find like-minded people amongst your friends, or even if you do not have any at the moment, you can always start off by looking up support groups on the internet. It is anonymous and it can be a very good first step for you to build up your self-esteem.

The only warning concerning this is: while the internet is filled with groups of people that can be supportive of you in your journey of self-development, it is equally full of people who do not care nor want to help anybody. Avoid at all costs groups of people that are in a constant negative dwelling place where they do nothing else but pity, criticize, and brood over their problems.

With the right individuals around you, you will notice how much faster you can grow. You will also notice how your own positive attitude helps others and builds confidence in both you and them.

6. Stay true to your purpose, but be flexible with your goals.

Once you have taken care of all the previous goals you will realize and start to embrace the fact that there are no goals that cannot be changed and nothing that you cannot be flexible with. As you move along you will start to redefine your goals and you will, by virtue of exposing yourself to new circumstances and gaining new knowledge about yourself, start to understand what works best for you in any particular circumstance.

Your own intuition will tell you what advices to take and what to ignore. You will no longer have a need for clearly set guidelines; instead you will find it in yourself to understand what you need to do. You will still be open-minded and listen to what other like-minded people are saying and doing, but you will be able to take their advice with a grain of salt.

As you set and reach your goals you will always continue to find new challenges. The more you develop, the more you will realize that it is the journey itself, the process that you are undertaking that is giving you joy.

Furthermore, stay observant and do not push yourself beyond where you truly are. If you notice that you might have missed something on one of the previous steps, be honest with yourself and go back to that stage of your development. There is nothing that is a bigger sign of maturity and confidence than admitting to yourself that you might have run past something without truly understanding it.

7. Share what you have overcome.

Once you feel mature and confident enough you will intuitively know that the time has come for you to take a step further on to helping others. This may express itself in different forms, but the fact remains that once you have broken through your old comfort zones and managed to fulfill many of your old goals you will -

without even thinking about it - begin to share your own experiences with others.

The moment you take on the role of an authority on a subject you will notice that you are not only teaching others, but that you are teaching yourself as well. The people that are the best in any given subject are the ones that are aware of their own strengths and weaknesses, and that never stop their own improvement and development, even though they appear to others as an authority.

Sharing the knowledge and wisdom that you have gained from your own development will in many ways be a catalyst for many good things. Your personal story will help others to find their courage in starting their own journeys.

6   JUST FOR THE GUYS : WHY THAT IS SO IMPORTANT

. . .

Women often cite confidence as the most attractive quality in a man. Why? When you're confident, nothing is out of reach, no goal is too lofty, and no challenge is too hard. A confident guy will do whatever it takes not only to survive, but to thrive and ensure his family and friends are well-cared for. He's not afraid to go after what he wants in life.

Many guys struggle with displaying confidence, especially if they're shy or don't have much experience with taking risks. Following are some improvements you can make in specific areas of your life— changes that will put a pep in your step and amplify your courage around women, around other men, and in your life, period.

Body Language

Strong body language is one of the most immediate indicators of confidence. Pay close attention to the way you normally carry yourself. Are you hunched over a lot? Do you slouch when you sit? Do you have a habit of keeping your eyes focused on the ground while walking, as if you're perpetually looking for lost coins or there's a 100-pound weight hanging on your neck?

If you're committing these body language faux pas, it's time to amend your ways. Fortunately, just knowing that there's a better way is the first step. Take it upon yourself to be aware of your posture in every situation.

You want to make sure that you're standing or sitting up straight, with your chest slightly elevated, facing straight ahead. When you walk, don't be afraid to take a slow, even pace and swing your arms at a normal rate. Work on these changes every day so that they become second nature, especially in the workplace and on dates.

Whether you're walking down the street or you're spending the day with a woman, these simple changes will make you appear more alert, focused, and energized. People will notice!

Exercise

Exercise isn't just for health freaks. It's a solid step towards boosting your confidence.

If you're even slightly out of shape and not that used to physical activity, now is the time to stop by your local gym and make regular exercise a part of your life. If you're not all that familiar with proper exercise routines, don't skip new member orientations or opportunities for personal training. Alternatively, you could also join an amateur sports league in your city.

Exercise will do great things for you. It will heighten your levels of naturally-occurring testosterone, which in of itself provides a boost of energy and confidence. If done properly, it will also improve your posture. You can guarantee it—once you're exercising regularly, others will take notice.

Eye Contact

One of the things that immediately separate the boys from the men is strength of eye contact. Looking people in the eye as you're talking to them can show without a doubt that you're someone to be reckoned with.

This doesn't mean you have to stare your coworkers down, or hold an unwavering gaze into a woman's eyes. That will make people uncomfortable. Instead, when you're introducing yourself or you're already in the midst of conversation, hold eye contact when the other person is talking and especially when you're talking. You can divert your eyes every now and then to take the pressure off the other person, but return full attention when the conversation picks up again.

You can even make use of your peepers in an incredibly confident move to approach women—simply lock eyes with someone you're attracted to until she notices you. If she smiles and shyly looks down, there's a good chance she's into it and would like to meet you!

Taking Initiative

Taking initiative is the hallmark of successful people. Going after what you want can bring you the kind of love life, financial independence, and freedom you long for. Others are naturally drawn to people that take initiative.

You can start by making small changes in your life. If you've been on the job for a few years and you honestly feel you deserve a promotion, set up a meeting with your supervisor today. If there's a woman in your life that you're interested in, call her up and ask her out today. If there's a certain new skill you want to learn, sign up for some classes today. Added bonus, you may just meet someone special!

Putting your own feet to the fire is necessary because it's too easy to let everyday life get in the way of your dreams and goals. The thought of shaking things up might make you nervous because it requires you to leave your comfort zone. However, if you fail to act, weeks, months, and years can go by, and you're still in the same position as before—unsatisfied with the status quo of your life. If there's a change you want to make, start taking steps toward it now. Get into an action-taking frame of mind and unshakeable confidence will follow.

Having Fun

Perhaps you've heard the popular saying "All work and no play makes Jack a dull boy." Well, it's true. If you're not taking the time to have a little fun, chances are you won't feel energized, refreshed, and ready for the more challenging or boring aspects of daily life. You won't be able to harness that confident spontaneity that comes with an active recreational life.

Fortunately, you can start to have more fun by doing things you like or might like, whether that's learning how to play guitar or how to play soccer. Take up an extreme sport or hang out with your friends at a karaoke bar.

Anything that makes you drop your inhibitions, gets you moving, and is just downright fun is something that can round off your character and builds your self-esteem in the long run. Let's face it; we all like to be around people who are fun to be around. High self-esteem (that is not on the conceited side) is something we all need to have and it is very attractive in a partner. No one wants to spend their time with a Danny-downer!

Summary

Becoming more confident is a challenge everyone should take on. It is a journey that will enhance your love life, boost your chances for financial success, and make you an all-around solid rock that others can rely on. The best part of the deal is that you can start taking charge of your life right now. I have given you the steps in this book. Take it slow, take a leap, whatever works for you but you have to take that first step. Go to the mirror now. On your way to the mirror envision who you want to be and when you step in front of the mirror, see that person. Now remember that person, remember how you felt and looked and the next time you head out that door, take that feeling and look with you. You might just be amazed at how a small change in your posture or a smile can make a big change in how you feel and how other see you.

Only one question remains—what are you waiting for?

The Most Important Thing You Can Do To Spread The Word

I thank you for reading my book.

If I may just ask if you could spare me just a few minutes of your precious time, to **LEAVE A REVIEW TODAY** if you have indeed enjoyed reading the stories in this book.

If you could, please help to spread the word around by leaving a review.

WHY REVIEWS MATTER

It is every writer's desire to have their book being held in the hands of readers such as you, and to share in the writer's belief in the stories.

As it is a very competitive environment out there in the publishing world, with many writers wanting to be noticed, asking for reviews is one of the most pragmatic ways we can gain more readers to share in our stories.

It is through getting and reading reviews from you, that writers like me get encouraged and to be spurred in writing more exciting stories to share with all of you.

Will You Be a Part of Our 1%?

The truth of the matter is, many who read a book seldom review it. In fact, less than 1% of them do.

Reasons for not leaving a review are plentiful….

Some say it is too tedious to write.

Some have absolutely no idea what to write.

For some, it never even came cross their mind to review the book.

Or they simply claim it is a waste of their time.

If you truly do not wish to review my book, I totally understand. You have already blessed my heart by reading my book, and I thank you for that.

If however, you choose to belong to that 1% readers who are willing to lend writers a helping hand, to help us get noticed, it will be most ideal.

Indie authors such as us seek audience and it is through word-of-mouth and reviews at Amazon, Apple, Barnes & Nobel, Goodreads, and similar sites that can make all the difference in the world between whether a new reader will find and buy our books.

All I need is just a few minutes and it would have made a **huge difference** in how indie writers' stories will unfold.

Your words need not be long. Just honest words, truthful feedback of the reasons why you enjoyed reading the book and this would mean the world to me.

Please go to the Amazon page for the book that you wish to review.

Thank you for reading.

~ Alan Kensington

ABOUT THE AUTHOR

For many years Alan struggled to develop his own personality issues, not being able to communicate effectively with others. This was due to his lack of self-confidence and he needed to find a way around it.

Alan began reading books from all over the globe trying to find a way to boost his esteem, confidence and he just wanted to be more sure of himself, to stop second guessing his own decisions and to be able to move forward as his own man. Alan realized that no one method could give you self-confidence and his book covers all of these strategies.

www.ingramcontent.com/pod-product-compliance
Ingram Content Group UK Ltd.
Pitfield, Milton Keynes, MK11 3LW, UK
UKHW022119230426
12048UKWH00010BA/614